Ishbel McFarlane

O is for Hoolet

&

Concise Scots Stories

Salamander Street

PLAYS

First published in 2020 by Salamander Street Ltd.
(info@salamanderstreet.com)

Printed and bound in Great Britain

10 9 8 7 6 5 4 3 2 1

Thanks

My thanks go to Vanessa Coffey and Ros Sydney for their help in creating *Hoolet*. Thanks to the Arches (RIP) for their support – *Hoolet* was the last show made in that building – and to Jill Smith and Kat Boyle of Feral for dusting off the wreckage and taking us on the road for many years. Thanks to Heloise Allan for her help with my school-girl French, to my dad for his help with my previously-abandoned Scots, and to my mum for shedding her shame about Jock and seeing the show dozens of times. And thanks, finally and always, to Tommy.

For Irene Russell and Maria Harley

Funders and partners
The Arches
Corrymeela Community
Creative Scotland
DeafAction
Dumfries and Galloway Arts Festival
Fèisean nan Gàidheal
North East Arts Touring
Scottish Government
Scots Language Centre
Scottish Storytelling Centre
Traverse Theatre
Ulster Scots Foundation

Produced by The Arches (2014-15) and Feral (2015-)

INTRODUCTION

I made *O is for Hoolet* in a huff. I started my professional life as an academic and researcher – using the word ontological more than anyone needs to, if we're honest. In 2009 I abandoned this path and moved to Glasgow to study acting – a choice my supervisor described as 'running away to join the circus'. Four years later I was a twenty-eight-year-old actor and had finally decided that it was time I addressed my relationship with Scots, which had reared its head in my academic days. The best way I knew how to explore complex ideas was to make a play about them. I wanted to find my path through a hundred thousand voices and opinions that had been swirling around me for more than twenty years. I applied to make the show at the Arches in Glasgow, was turned down, but was invited to make a twenty minute scratch (work in progress) instead. I did not want to make a 'scratch'. I did not want twenty minutes. I had twenty years of stuff and I was in a huff.

But I did it – an empty stage does focus the mind. My friend, Vanessa Coffey, worked with me as dramaturg and helped me to find a way to wrangle the voices into something which kept a flavour of them in fragments and constant questions. I worked hard to make the internal, the political and the academic into something theatrical. To make a play. The scratch led to the Platform 18 award, a full production the following year, and then a national tour the year after that. And I've been performing it, in one form or another, ever since.

At the start of the tour we did a show at Platform, in Easterhouse, to a packed, theatre-savvy, festival audience. Full lights, dressing room, lots of space. The show went down really well. The following day we did it for the community centre in Dalmarnock to half a dozen folk behind tables for their teacakes and juice – us fitting in the set around them, and my crew taking much of the audience participation. I had wanted to make a show that was flexible and could be done anywhere, and Dalmarnock Community Centre was our first big stretch. The show involves lots of reading, lots of academic references, lots of my unconscious presumptions. But we made it through. I sang my song. We got a round of applause. I felt our wee play could go anywhere and do anything. As we were packing up so they could get on with the dominoes one audience member said to Sarah, the stage manager, 'Ishbel is really good. She should be an actor.' Oh-sha, thon's burnie.

I don't want to disappoint that lady, but *O is for Hoolet* made me not an actor, but an activist. When I read it now I see in it the academic I had been, the actor I was and the activist I became. Finding a way to articulate my story, hearing the stories that other people share with me, and relearning Scots – these things made me an activist. I still have innumerable questions, but I am in a different place with Scots now than when I wrote it. And so is Scots itself. In the summer of 2014 there was no way to have a qualification in Scots – a fact which bewildered the minority language academics and campaigners I spoke to in other countries. Now there are SQA awards up to Higher equivalent. The Open University has a Scots Language course which, at the time of writing, is one of the most popular courses ever on their website. There are moves to have a Scots Language Board, the language is increasingly visible in the linguistic landscape, and Scots was enthusiastically included in celebrations of the UN's Year of Indigenous Langauges in 2019. When you ask Google 'What is Scots language?' it no longer answers, 'English'. Things are changing. But when I perform *Hoolet* there are always, always, always people in the audience who have never considered any of the issues discussed at all. We're not done. Scots is not done. We're no duin yet.

Ishbel McFarlane, January 2020

PERFORMANCE NOTES

O is for Hoolet is a partly-interactive performance. Just partly. There is flexibility to make slight changes for the context of each performance, and the answers I give as myself are fluid around set ideas. However, the script as you read it is always performed in the same order, with the audience asking questions I provide on bits of card. The aim of this technique is to let the audience feel they as if they are having the start of a discussion which they want to continue when they leave the room. Writing their own questions at the start encourages them to assess their starting relationship with Scots so they can easier identify any shifts by the end. All of these techniques are part of a pedagogical drive in the show. It is, however, not a lecture. It is a play.

Hi there, thanks for coming. Welcome – my name is Ishbel McFarlane and I'm going to be performing the show today. The show, as you might know, is called *O is for Hoolet*. You'll find out why it's called that during the next hour or so. I wanted to greet you and give you a heads up that there will be audience participation in the show, but that that participation is not compulsory. There will be a chance for people to read things out during the show, but if you don't want to, you don't have to. There will be plenty of show offs in this room. What I would love everyone to do though is to have a think before we start. To have a think about Scots language, which is sometimes also called Scots dialect, or Scots slang, or Doric, or Fife dialect or Glaswegian, or the way we speak in Dumfries, or a whole range of other names, and, using the cards and pencils you got as you came in, to write down one question that you have about Scots. It can be about anything to do with Scots, from a very specific question about the meaning of a word, all the way to a huge sweeping question about the socio-political challenges of Scots. No-one needs to see what you write down, so don't worry about spelling or being 'correct'. I'm going to have a sit down and give you a few minutes to have a write and then we'll get started, Is that okay? Great.

Ishbel sits and waits for three or four minutes.

I think you've mostly finished. If you wrote down a question could you hold up your card for me now so I can see them? Wonderful. An excellent union meeting – the motion passes! Could I ask you now to take your card and put it under your bahookie? You can put it under your seat if you'd rather not go anywhere near your bahookie. We'll come back to those much later, you can forget about them for now.

That lovely wee forest of cards showed that you have a few questions about Scots language. When I was starting to try to understand my own personal experiences with Scots, I started with some questions too, and I wrote them down. I had a bit longer than you so I wrote quite a few. Here's the audience participation I told you about – because I am doing a one-woman show about language and language is inherently social, I need people to talk with – that's youse. Each of my pink cards has one or two questions typed on it, and I am going to hand them out to you in the audience. If you are willing, I would like you to take a card and read the question out – weirdly loudly – at a specific point in the show. I will then try to answer your question using my memories, opinions, experiences, by using the books I have on stage, by playing different characters, all to get an overarching view of Scots. You will know who I am playing because each question is addressed to that character. So this one says, 'Ishbel, what languages do you speak?' so you'd read that whole thing out and you'd know I'd be playing myself, Ishbel. But it could also read 'Theresa May, what's your favourite Scots word?' and then I would be playing Theresa May and we'd all laugh.

You will know when it's your turn to read your question out by our absolutely ingenious bingo-style number system. Each question has a number next to it, and also, in true belt-and-braces style, has that same number on the back of the card. When it's time for you to speak, your number will come up on this screen here, and belt-and-braces again, it'll come over the tannoy with me doing my best ScotRail voice. Let's check you can see and hear that now.

Tests.

Beware, in true bingo-style, the numbers are not in numerical order, so you have to keep your eye on the game. Fun and terrifying!

I am going to hand these out now. If you don't want to read one out, that is okay, just pass it along. It doesn't matter if someone ends up with more than one card. When you get a card, have a little read of what it says, check the words. I'm going to start handing out at the back.

Hands out the question cards.

Is everyone who has a card happy that they have a card? Do we all know what's happening? Remember to be weirdly loud when you read your question out so even the people behind can hear you. It'll be fine.

Okay, let's go.

The number 1 appears on the screen and in voice over, prompting the appropriate audience member to read their question aloud.

1: Ishbel, what languages do you speak?

Ah, c'est un peu complique ça, non? Donc je parle l'anglais, bien sûr, en fait c'est l'anglais écossais. J'ai etudié le francais a l'école. Maintenant j'étudie la langue des signes britanniques. A la maison on parle l'écossais, ma mère et mon père toujours parlent l'écossais. Je ne pouvais pas parler l'écossais au kindergarten, c'etait interdit – à cause des profs, des autres parents et des enfants aussi, mes amis, oui. Donc je ne voulais pas parler l'écossais. Je ne permettais pas mes parents de parler l'écossais non plus. Et donc, de quelque part, je le reprends, ou, je le reprends d'avoir l'assurance de le parler.

4: Ishbel, what is a language?

Language is a code we use to get what is in our heads into the heads of other people.

5: Geoffrey Finch, author of 'Linguistic Terms and Concepts', that answer seemed fairly partial. She didn't split the word 'language' into Saussure's sections – langage, parole, langue – it's almost as if she only skimmed the reading in her first year English seminars. Rather than getting into all of that just now, could you explain what a code is?

In its simplest sense a code is a system of rules which allows us to transmit information in symbolic form. By this definition language is a code. It consists of words which symbolically represent ideas, events, and objects in the world outside, and which, when put together in certain sequences, enable us to communicate.

15: David Crystal, linguist and linguistic historian, what is the difference between a language and a dialect?

In brief, [As ISHBEL: which is much easier for David to do than it is for me to do], on purely linguistic grounds, two speech systems are considered to be dialects of the same language if they are *(predominantly)* mutually intelligible. On the other hand, purely linguistic considerations can be 'outranked' by sociopolitical criteria. A recent example is *Serbo-Croation*, formerly widely used as a language name to encompass a set of varieties used within former Yugoslavia, but following the civil wars of the 1990s now largely replaced by the names *Serbian*, *Croatian*, and *Bosnian*. In 1990 there was a single language spoken in these countries; now, despite the fact there's been little or no linguistic change, there are three.

18: Robert Burns, by letter dated September 1793, could you tell me about anything that you are working on just now?

The evening before last I wandered out, and began a tender song, in what I think its native style. I must premise that the old way, and the way to give most effect, is to have no starting note, as the fiddlers call it, but to burst at once into the pathos. My song is just begun; and I should like, before I proceed, to know your opinion of it. I have sprinkled it with the Scottish dialect, but it may be easily turned into correct English.

2: Ishbel, what languages do you speak?

Ishbel signs beginner-level British Sign Language.

- HARD

- SPEAK ENGLISH, SCOTTISH-ENGLISH

- SCHOOL LEARN FRENCH – NOW LEARN SIGN

- PAST GROWING HOME SPEAK SCOTS, MUM–DAD ALWAYS TALK SCOTS

- NURSERY (TOPIC) SCOTS BAD, NOT AT ALL NEVER – OTHER PARENTS, TEACHERS, MY FRIENDS

- DIDN'T WANT SCOTS – MUM–DAD SPOKE SCOTS, I IGNORED

- NOW SCOTS (TOPIC), AGAIN LEARN OR MAYBE AGAIN LEARN CONFIDENCE TO SPEAK.

37: Ishbel, what inspired you to explore Scots language on stage?

So. About a decade ago *(which is horrific)* I was a student at the School of Scottish Studies at Edinburgh University studying Scottish Ethnology, and I was doing a project where I had to use the school's sound archive. So I went along to the catalogue room, which is a room that is about the size of this stage, but along one whole wall of this wee room are these little metal drawers with wee metal handles and each with a bit of paper on, telling you what's in the drawer. And inside the drawers were postcard-sized cards with fine lines on them, telling you what was in the archive. And thus, children, was Google of the olden days.

I had no idea where to start in this closed wall of stuff, so I did that typically egocentrical, ethnological thing and thought 'I'll start with where I'm from'. So I went to the drawer that has Kinross in it, which is where I'm from. I say IN it, because Kinross is not important enough to have a drawer of its own. It has to share with other humiliating places like Clackmannan. So I found the drawer and I looked through every single card in the Kinross section. Some of them are pink and that shows you there's a sound holding in the archive about that thing, and some are white, and that shows you there's a written holding in the archive about that thing. So I look through every single one, and I find a pink one that says: Irene Russell, 1971, Jock o Hazeldean.

Irene Russell was my mum's maiden name, and in 1971 she would have been nineteen, the same age I was looking at this card. And although she's not a professional singer, she's always sung, and I know that Jock o Hazeldean is a song, so this could viably be a recording of my mum singing. So I take the card to the archivist and he goes down into the bowels of the building and gets the reel-to-reel recorder, and puts the tape on, and we watch it go round and round and there, completely recognisably, from thirty-five years in the past, comes the sound of my nineteen-year-old mum singing. It was like a miracle! I had never heard of this recording and I was pretty sure my mum didn't even know it existed.

In the recording she's singing this song, Jock o Hazeldean, which was written, or collected, by Sir Walter Scott. So it's a Borders song. It's about a young girl who has been promised to marry the English lord of the manor, Frank of Errington, who has everything you could want in a husband – primarily dance skills and a wonderful sword. But she keeps crying and crying because she's in love with Jock o Hazeldean, the Scottish, Jack the lad character. At the end of the song, it's her wedding day, and the lord and the priest and all the guests are waiting, but she's nowhere to be found because she's away over the border with Jock o Hazeldean. From an ethnographic perspective it's quite interesting because it's a rare example of a folk song which ends happily for a woman.

I got the track put on to a CD, I immediately took it home and uploaded it onto my computer and I burned it onto a mixed CD for my mum's birthday, which was coming up. But I didn't mention the track on the track listing, because I understand the power of a hidden track. Ever since Robbie Williams' Life Thru *(with a U)* a Lens.

I went home for Christmas, which is when her birthday is, and on her birthday I set the table all nice and I wrapped the CD, and I wait for her to come through. When she does she opens the CD and she says, 'oh, thanks Ishbel, that's very nice' and I'm like, 'yeah no bother Mum' playing it cool. And we're just chatting and having our breakfast and then I say, 'Mum, why don't we listen to that CD the now? I just happen to have a CD player here, open, plugged in, switched on, ready to go' and Mum was like, 'Yeah, fine, sounds good.' So I put the CD in, and press play.

Now the first track's something else, something we both love, like The Lark Ascending, and we're just chatting and having our cereal. Then that track finishes and there's that wee pause when one track ends, before the next track starts, and I'm like that *[poses]*, watching her. At first when the singing starts she doesn't recognise it, why would she, then

she stops,

she listens,

she realises

and she goes oh noooo! Which is not the response anyone wants to a surprise birthday present.

So it turns out that the recording was done without my mum's knowledge at a folk festival in Kinross, and Mum had never done anything like that before and she was nervous, and she made a wee mistake. And, as with all strong, Scottish emotions, she had buried that humiliating memory deep within her. And here it was, on her birthday, right back up on the breakfast table.

What I couldn't make her understand, though, was that that is my favourite bit. When she's singing she sounds exactly like herself, totally recognisably my mum. But when she goes back and has to correct her words she goes: huh, sorry. Just like that! Exactly like me! Exactly like I will probably do at some point during the show today if I make a mistake. I couldn't even hear my mum in that, all I could hear was myself, especially when I was nineteen, and so it was this amazing gift of nineteen-year-old Irene Russell holding her hand out to nineteen-year-old Ishbel McFarlane and saying, 'Yeah, me too'.

But worse than that for my mum, worse than the mistake, was that she'd gone along to this folk festival knowing nothing about the folk revival that Scotland had been going through over the last decades. The festival moved around Scotland each year, and it happened to be in Kinross that year. Though my pal, Scott, who is still involved in the festival says it's not so much that it moved around Scotland, more that it was repeatedly chucked out of places. So in 1971 it was in Kinross and mum had never been to a folk festival, but she liked singing because the one teacher in her one teacher school, Miss Noble, had said to my grandma, 'Oh, Mrs Russell, Irene's got a lovely voice, maybe she should have a singing lesson'. So she'd had lessons here and there and she's got this semi-trained, semi-operatic, sort of English Song School style voice. And as she's on the stage performing, the people in the audience let her know that she is doing it wrong. That what she's bringing to that stage has no value. What's valued there is a sort of authenticity – a gritty connection with an oral culture that stretches back generations. And even though she was brought up on a farm in the 1950s, in rural Scotland, with a father who had followed a plough behind horses and watched his own father seeding grain by hand, she had been so removed from her culture that she didn't know how to perform it. And here she was, thirty-five years later, still deeply ashamed of that. And that just fascinated me. And it broke my heart.

38: Ishbel, can we hear that recording?

Yes.

Recording plays.

19: CPG, what is your group name, in line with the Code of Conduct 6.2.4?

Cross-Party Group *(or CPG)* in the Scottish Parliament on Scots Language

20: CPG, what is your group purpose, in line with the Code of Conduct 6.2.3 and 6.4, Rule 1?

To promote the cause of Scots, inform members of the culture and heritage of the language and highlight the need for action to support Scots.

21: CPG, could you provide details of your most recent meetings?

There have been no meetings since 2012. The abeyance of the meetings in 2013 was due to a discussion during the December 2012 meeting regarding the future direction of the CPG. Some discussions with the Scots Language Learning Centre about the likely direction of our work have dragged on and have still to be resolved. The CPG's aims have been met. E.g. progress in the past two years includes: The first time a question was asked in the census of 2011 regarding people's understanding and practising of the Scots language.

8: Parliament of 1567, you have an infant King James VI and a troublesome Queen Mary Stuart. How is the nation coping?

Presenting of the quenis majesteis commissionie

Marie, be the grace of God quene of Scottis, to all and sindry our jugeis and ministeris of law, liegis and subdittis quhome it efferis quhais knawlege thir oure lettres sal to cum, greting. Forsamekill as sen our arryvall and returning within oure realme, we, willing the commoun commoditie, welth, proffeit and quietnes thairof, liegis and subjectis of the samyn, haif employit oure body, haill sences and forceis to governe the same in sic sort that oure royall and honorabill estait mycht stand, continew with us and our posteritie, and our loving and kynd liegis mycht enjoy the quietnes of trew subjectis; in travelling quhairin nocht onelie is oure body, spreit and sences sa vexit, brokin and unquietit that langar we ar nocht of habilitie be ony maner to induir sa greit and in tollerabill panis and travellis quhairwith we ar altogidder weryit, bot als greit commotionis and troublis be sindry occasionis in the menetyme hes insewit thairin to oure greit greif.

24: Johann Wolfgang Unger, Scots language researcher at Lancaster University, what is habitus?

I think you should probably ask that question to the originator of the term, the dead, French sociologist and philosopher, Pierre Bordieu.

13: Pierre Bordieu, dead, French sociologist and philosopher, what is habitus?

In 'Allo 'Allo! levels of French accent.

That which one has acquired, but which has become durably incorporated into the body in the form of permanent dispositions.

23: Ishbel, what?

Yeah. So habitus is a theoretical term, devised by Pierre Bordieu, which comes from the Latin habere which means have, hold, or possess, which shifts and changes and becomes habitare – which means to live or dwell. Like in Scots and English we have inhabit, if you inhabit somewhere, you live there, you dwell there. But this habitus habitation is inside us and it has to do with our habitual structures of disposition. Which is difficult to describe with words.

Moves behind table and takes from the set one of the model houses with a book as a roof.

Let's use this handy wee hoose as a visual representation. I'm going to start by taking the roof off the hoose as a visual metaphor for looking inside the concept. That's theatre, ladies and gentlemen. And we'll need some bits and pieces to help with the metaphor, so does anyone have any small objects in a pocket that I can use on stage? So, kirbies or a watch, or a hairbrush or anything? [*Gathers five or so things from the audience*]. If you want these things back, you're going to have to come and get them at the end of the show or I will pochle them.

So for Bordieu, your habitus, the place where you live inside yourself, is created by everything that comes into you from the outside, everything you acquire. I'm going to use these objects to represent these, your experiences. So that includes *[holds up objects to represent each thing and puts them in the house]* things people say to you, things you see on social media, things you see advertised, things you overhear. All of that goes into you and that creates your habitus, and inside us, each experience bounces off the other experiences. And, then, for Bordieu, everything we give out into the world comes from this place, which was built by our experiences. So that could be *[takes objects out of the house one at a time and puts them beside the house]* the things you say, the way you vote in elections, the way you spend your money, the pictures you post on social media. Absolutely everything you give out into the world comes from this place, that was built by your experiences.

Now, there's a close relationship between a person's experiences and their attitudes *[puts same object through the journey of formation-habitus-generation]* – so maybe someone says something to you and then you repeat it, verbatim, to someone else. But you can't always predict it – sometimes what goes into us and what comes out of us are vastly different *[swaps the object in the house for a cat model – rapturous applause].* That's another central idea in habitus – even if you could know every experience a person has had, you can't always predict how they will think or act because of the way the experiences bounce off each other.

I first came across the concept of habitus in this book by Johann Wolfgang Unger, the Austrian guy who fobbed you off there to dead French Pierre Bordieu, *The Discursive Construction of the Scots Language* – it's basically a beach read. In this book Unger uses the example of a school age child to demonstrate habitus, we can call her Maria, because that's a lovely name, and it's also my middle name and it's also my mum's mum's name. *[Choosing a long object, puts it through the journey of formation-habitus-generation]* In the story Maria is belted at the school every time she uses a Scots word, and that goes into her habitus, it's part of her experience. Maria might flinch when she hears Scots spoken, but that alone isn't her habitus, that's almost an instinctual reaction, like Pavlov's dog. To make up her habitus you need to think about long-term socialisation and thousands and thousands of other things that went into her: the things her other teachers say to her, what she sees her parents doing, what she hears on the wireless, the jokes her big sister makes and so on and so on. All of that goes into her and creates her habitus. And in the story, when she grows up, Maria corrects her children when they use Scots words, she tells them to talk properly. We might say that Maria's performed actions reproduce the values which were violently forced on her as a child.

But the thing about habitus, as we have seen with the cat, is that it is not predictable. Maybe there's another wee girl sitting next to Maria at the school, let's call her Irene, and she was belted just as much as Maria, every time she used a Scots word. And that goes into her habitus along with everything else. But when Irene grows up she maybe doesn't correct her family when they use Scots, but becomes a Scots language campaigner. And maybe she encourages her daughter to make a show about Scots, touring festivals in summer 2017. For example. The handy thing about habitus is that not only does it help us explore individual attitudes, but also helps us examine a whole nation or culture. It's tempting to say, what is the reason Scots declined? Was it Union of the Crowns goes in and *Scots declined* comes out?

But with habitus we realise it's so much more complicated than that: we have to think about millions upon millions of tiny actions over generations, some repeating each other, some bouncing off each other in unexpected ways.

Habitus links experiences and attitudes without having to say A equals B in every case. We don't always have to tell the same, sad story.

Right, if you want my advice, I think you should ask Unger some more questions. You might want to ask him about the concept of violence and language a bit more. I don't know about you, but I wasn't strapped for using Scots at school, but here I am speaking English. Or maybe you just want a summary of his work on Scots. I'm not going to rush you, dae it in yer ain time.

9: Jean Redpath, folk singer and educator, were you encouraged to sing in the hoose and at the school?

That's twa afie different questions! In the hoose – aye. Eh there was ey music o some kind. My mither did a lot o singin, ma faither played the dulcimer. At the schuil singin wis a nawfie different thing. Ye hud tae hae a bool in yer mooth there, an although A wis far too well [pause] trained an broucht up tae say, A'm no go dae that, eh, A niver really took tae it. A A A do, A do remember, with great sorrae, the one Scottish song, an ye'll notice the accent has changed because I'm working up to the hands clutched under the bosom approach to this stuff

which-eh, it took me years to realise this was a
Scots song at all:

Sings.

A Highland lad my love was born,
The Lowland laws he held in scorn;
But he still was faithful to his clan,
My gallant braw John Highlandman.

D'ye no think if that's a, an accurate picture o
the eichteenth-century highlanders, nae wonder
we lost the Jacobite uprisins?

16: David Crystal, why is it important
to discuss language death?

I'm glad you ask me that. I believe it is vitally
important. [As ISHBEL: More vitally important
even than David's phenomenal beard and
glasses]. I recall, in early 1997, writing a piece for
the *Guardian* about my *(at the time)* forthcoming
book, *English as a Global Language*. Imagine, I
said, what could happen if English continues
to grow as it has. Maybe one day it will be the
only language left to learn. If that happens, I
concluded, it will be the greatest intellectual
disaster that the planet has ever known.

6: Geoffrey Finch, why should we be saving Scots when it is just a dialect, and not a language, like English or French?

It's important to bear in mind that the term 'dialect' is purely descriptive. There is no implication that one variety is in any sense better than any other. However, people often have their own preferences and will frequently seek to exalt these into judgements about linguistic correctness. The issue of 'correctness' arises particularly in relation to standard English, which is popularly regarded as not a dialect, because of its national status and its non-regional character. Historically speaking, however, the basis of what is now standard English was the local dialect of the region bounded by Oxford, Cambridge, and London. Its elevation has been the consequence of a number of social and cultural factors, but these shouldn't hide from us the fact that it is still a variety of the language, albeit a non-regional and socially normative one, and therefore Standard English itself can still be thought of as a dialect.

25: Johann Wolfgang Unger, I think we're ready to explore some more of your stuff now. Will you give us a summary of some of your work on Scots?

I set up a series of focus groups to investigate how Scots speakers discursively construct their language and negotiate its many definitions and meanings in their lives. The focus groups were characterised by high levels of ambivalence towards Scots. Scots receives lavish praise on the one hand, but participants found it difficult to talk about, and were not used to reading it. The 'artificiality' of Scots in formal registers is compared with its 'authenticity' in the home or in the playground, with little recognition that the lack in one register might lead to the lack in all registers. That is not to say that the participants were ignorant of the decline in the use of Scots in their communities. However, it seems that since particular patterns of linguistic practices are deeply engrained in each participant's linguistic *habitus*, it is impossible for them to escape. They are full of *double-voiced* utterances. The world where Scots is unacceptable exists side-by-side inside their body with the world where it is to be valued.

14: Dr Alasdair Allan MSP, you were the Scottish Government's Minister for Learning, Science and Scotland's Languages, and you were the first person to hold such a post who is a Scots speaker. What are your aims for Scots language?

A dinna want oniebudy tae go through schuil withoot kennin that Scots exists, but aiblins mair important than yon, A don't want oniebody to go though schuil at his Scots believin it his nae value. An certainly ma ain experience i'the schuils, no so muckle in the primary schuil, but certainly the secondary schuil, was that Scots, an Scots literature an the Scots leid was somethin o nae accoont at aw.

36: Four-year-old Ishbel in 1990, can you read me your book?

Uh huh.

Collects alphabet book from the back of the stage and reads a page with drawings of mouse, newt and owl.

M is for moose, N is for newt, O is for hoolet.

Beat.

26: Johann Wolfgang Unger, could you explore the concept of violence in terms of language a wee bit more?

Symbolic violence is Pierre Bordieu's term and refers to the often unconscious every-day social habits of social and cultural domination. [As ISHBEL: You know when a man's taking up too much space on the bus, he's just pure manspreading all over the place, that's an example of symbolic violence. I say on the bus, but I could easily mean in the theatre.] The 'soft' nature of symbolic violence allows its violent nature to go unrecognised. Some participants in my focus groups are aware of the symbolic violence they see as being perpetrated against Scots and Scots speakers as a daily occurrence. They do not, however, have a toolkit of strategies to resist this violence. Rather, they mitigate, hesitate and negatively predicate Scots even while saying how important it is to them.

7: So, Geoffrey Finch, what is code-switching?

Code-switching is the shifting by speakers between one dialect, or language, and another. Many native English speakers will switch between speaking regional dialect, or non-standard English, casually among friends, and standard English for professional, or business, purposes. Bidialecticalism, as it is sometimes called, has received the overt support of many linguists as a way to approach the difficulty which schools face of giving appropriate recognition to the local dialect of children whilst at the same time respecting their entitlement to acquire standard English.

17: David Crystal, the internet is changing the way we use language. Do you think it is having any influence on Scots?

I mean, to what extent is the internet actually being used by Scots young people, people, young people who are using Scots and who are as it were, letting their fingers dictate the way in which they feel Scots should be spelled. Now this is an alternative institution to the ones we were talking about before. It isn't now some academic sitting in W & R Chambers saying, 'Here is the Scots dictionary, and these are the spellings you should use'. To heck with him. Now the internet is producing millions more examples of Scots than was ever in the Scots dictionary corpus, and so what's going to happen here? I don't know the answer to that, but I see the future of Scots being very much bound up with the future of the internet in Scotland.

10: Google, what is your answer to the query, 'What is Scots Language?'?

"English"

27: But, friend of a friend, do you not think that it's important to tell the wee kids that you teach that the way they speak is alright? That it's valid?

It's alright at home. They can speak like that to their parents. Or in the playground. But I won't have them in my classroom sayin – I mean, I have kids in that class who are incapable of saying mum. Ma maw, ma maaaaaw. I say to them, your what? What's that? Maw? It drives me up the wall. It's my job to prepare them for work. If they walk into an interview speaking like that no one's going to take them seriously. Maw. I mean, I won't let them swear in the classroom either – it's just the same.

28: But, friend of a friend, my parents brought me up speaking Scots, I wasn't allowed to speak it at school or playgroup, and I think it has a serious effect on whether you feel like your voice should be heard. The kids you teach are nine or ten years old, don't you think it's more important to make them feel like their thoughts matter?

Listen, I don't know you, Ishbel, but I think you probably had access to English too and good education and middle-class things that those kids don't have. I have kids in that class who can't read CVC words. That's consonant vowel consonant – cat, bat, mat. They have to leave my classroom able to read and not to be judged by folk who they meet for sounding thick. I don't make the system. It's not fair to prepare those kids for a world that doesn't exist, where people don't judge them if they use the word maw instead of the proper English word.

11: Seventeen-year-old Ishbel in 2004, what did you get for your Christmas?

Shut up! I didn't ask to be born. I hate you. You don't understand me. I'm going to my room to listen to Evanescence.

39: Ishbel, is that actually what you were like when you were seventeen?

No.

12: Actual seventeen-year-old Ishbel in 2004, what did you get for your Christmas?

Three different people gave me copies of *Eats, Shoots, and Leaves: A Zero Tolerance Approach to Punctuation* by Lynne Truss, because everyone knows I'm a grammar nazi. [As ISHBEL: By the way, if you were given the book *Eats, Shoots and Leaves* with the phrase 'I knew you'd love this' or 'this really reminded me of you', that means you're a dick.] I think it's really important to use correct grammar, spelling and punctuation. I love reading and I love poetry and, for the last two years, I've won the slightly unfortunately named Hoare Reading Prize at my school. And I was also the World Burns Federation Recitation Champion. So that's quite good. I think Scots is really important, and I love the poetry that I learn and recite in it, but I would never write it because I don't know the rules. I pride myself in being able to speak in interviews, and I am confident that I sound like a well-rounded, well-spoken young girl. I have a Gaelic name, but I don't speak any Gaelic, but I wish I could because I think it would kind of like, complete me. I correct my friends on their English usage, which I am trying not to because nobody likes bossy girls. I am bad at spelling and maybe a bit dyslexic, which worries and embarrasses me. I'm dreading going to uni and into the real world, and I love school, and I know that's partly because I do know the rules here – I mean that figuratively and literally. Sometimes I read the school rules in bed before I go to sleep.

Everyone thinks teenagers are rule breakers, but we're not. Like, when Mr Salisbury moved his English classroom around, everyone in my class went totally radgey. We like to conform – not to everything, obviously, but definitely to each other. We hate change. That seems very clear to me.

Oh, and I'm not nearly as together as thirty-one-year-old Ishbel seems to think I am. And I wouldn't use the word radgey. I stopped using it when I was thirteen because Mr McCann found it funny when I used it once in hockey.

32: Scots Language Centre, what is Scots Language?

Scots is coontit a breench o the Germanic family o leids, an is, like its sister tongue Soothrin, sprung fae the auld Angles leid. Baith auld Angles, an its dauchter, Scots, has been spoken in soothlan an easter Scotland, the lallans, fae the siventh century AD. Thi're mentions o this leid tae be fund, fir instance, in the runic carvins oan the Rivell cross in Dumfrieshire, biggit in the echt century AD.

Scots shouldnae, o coorse, be taiglit wi Scots Gaelic – that's a Celtic tongue, an the sister leid o Eirse.

The first text in Scots tae win ower belangs the fourteenth century, though thi're are nummer

o Latin texts wi vernacular glosses in them that
dates back tae the twalt century.

34: Ishbel, what happens when you read the bible in Scots at your church?

Fowk greet.

35: Ishbel, why do you think that is?

Fowk his niver heard the words o their God,
wha steyed in the regional backwatter o Galilee,
speakin in the wey their mither an faither spak
tae them an the wey they speak tae their ain
bairns.

29: Slightly-older four-year-old Ishbel in 1991, will you come ben the hoose?

Mum, it's not hoose, it's house.

30: Slightly older four-year-old Ishbel, in oor language it's hoose. How come you say it isn't?

In my language it's house. Paula says so. Paula
is my best friend in playgroup.

40: Ishbel, do Scottish writers explore Scots language?

Aye they do.

This is Liz Lochhead

<u>Kidspoem/Bairnsang</u>

it wis January
and a gey dreich day
the first day Ah went to the school
so my Mum happed me up in ma
good navy-blue napp coat wi the rid tartan hood
birled a scarf aroon ma neck
pu'ed oan ma pixie an' my pawkies
it wis that bitter
said noo ye'll no starve
gie'd me a wee kiss and a kid-oan skelp oan the bum
and sent me aff across the playground
tae the place Ah'd learn to say
it was January
and a really dismal day
the first day I went to school
so my mother wrapped me up in my
best navy-blue top coat with the red tartan hood,
twirled a scarf around my neck,
pulled on my bobble-hat and mittens
it was so bitterly cold
said now you won't freeze to death
gave me a little kiss and a pretend slap on the bottom
and sent me off across the playground
to the place I'd learn to forget to say
it wis January
and a gey dreich day

the first day Ah went to the school
so my Mum happed me up in ma
good navy-blue napp coat wi the rid tartan hood,
birled a scarf aroon ma neck,
pu'ed oan ma pixie an' ma pawkies
it wis that bitter.

Oh saying it was one thing
but when it came to writing it
in black and white
the way it had to be said
was as if you were posh, grown-up, male,
English and dead.

33: Tom Leonard, will you tell us why it's important to legislate for Scots and to have official documents in an approved Scots?

He will no. Tom Leonard's a weel-kent established poet fae Glesga. His wark's political an aims for tae upset the status quo. His maist famous poems is phonetic renderins o West o Scotland speech, the best kent o thae is 'This is thi six o clock news'. Incidentally, 'Unrelated Incidents', which thon poem comes frae, pairtly inspirit the structure o this shaw.

Tom Leonard disnae believe in Scots Language. He believes that an attempt tae mak respect fir 'Scots' isnae an attempt tae free fowk frae the hegemony of Standart English, but an attempt tae mak a new hegemony tae which aw mon subscribe. Tom Leonard is feart o whit he cries internal colonisation, the takkin o language as spoken frae the mooths o the speakers, an tellin them tae conform tae a scrievit word. But, as ane o his poems pynts oot, it's no the word that wis in the beginnin, it wis the soon. An we micht add, the sign.

Jingso, A've nae answers tae the questions that Tom Leonard raises. No jist spierins aboot leid, but wha belangs leid, ken, the ownership o words. A've bin blyth tae inhabit ithers here – Burns, Crystal, Redpath, thon pal o a pal A met yince. A've taen scrievit words an made them spoken, taen spoken words an pit them in ma body so they cam frae ma mooth. It's gey temptin no tae explore thae issues at aw, but thir's muckle load of questions tae address. Gin A cannae ainser them, A'll jist add ma ain. Here's some spierins aboot whit Tom Leonard sis:

1) Is there nae road tae learn folk a leid that aye welcomes variation?

2) Can ye ettle tae inhabit anither body wioot exertin pooer ower that body?

3) Whan will we cam tae a place whaur we realise that the scrievit leid is a yaisefu tool tae

communicate soons an signs, an no the maister
that dictates oor spoken or signed leid? It's pairt
o the hoose, no the hale jing – bang.

**31: Audience, get out the questions that you
wrote at the start of the show. [READER OF THE
QUESTION: pause here to give the audience time
to do this.] Ishbel is going to answer one of your
questions the now. Will you put your hand up if you
feel like your question hasn't been answered yet
and you would like to ask it aloud?**

*An audience member then asks a question and Ishbel answers it using the
books on the stage and her own opinions. A selection can be found from page
39 of this book.*

*After the question is answered, Ishbel will let everyone know that if they feel
like their question hasn't been answered they can put it in the box and she
will answer some of them online. People can look it up on oisforhoolet.com.*

3: Ishbel, what languages do you speak?

Ach, that's a bittie complicatit. Eh, so obviously
A speak Inglis, eh sortie Scots-Inglis. Eh, I learnt
French at the schuil. The noo A'm learnin –
learnin British Sign Leid. But A was brocht
up speakin Scots, ma mither an faither aye
deliberately spak Scots tae me. Bit A wisnae
allowed tae speak it at nursery or the playgroup,

eh, by the staff, or ither mithers and faithers
or by ma pals, an sae A didnae want to speak
an A deliberately didnae want to speak it an A
wouldnae let ma mither an faither speak it an
aw. An sae in some weys, A doot, A'm re-learnin
it, or re-learning the confidence ta speak it.

41: How would you sing Jock o Hazeldean, Ishbel?

Goes to start, but stumbles.

Eh, sorry.

Sings.

Why weep ye by the tide lady,
Why weep ye by the tide,
I'll wed ye tae my youngest son,
And ye shall be his bride.
And ye shall be his bride lady,
Sae comely tae be seen,
But aye she luit the tears doon fa
For Jock o Hazeldean.

Noo let this willfu greif be done,
And dry thy cheek so pale.
Young Frank is Chief of Errington,
And Lord o Langleydale,
His step is first in peacefu ha,

His sword in battle keen,
But aye she luit the tears doon fa
For Jock o Hazeldean.

The kirk was decked at morning tide,
The tapers glimmered fair,
The priest and bridegroom wait the bride,
And dame and knight are there,
They socht her baith in bower and ha
The lady wasna seen,
She's ower the border and awa,
Wi Jock o Hazeldean.

Audience Questions

On my blog oisforhoolet.com I answered some of the questions that audience members submitted but which there wasn't time to answer in the show.

I reproduce a selection of those questions and answers here so you can get an idea of the sorts of questions that people had, and the sorts of answers I gave in the room. I have included the date when the question was submitted – many of my answers would be different now. The posts are printed as they appeared on the website, apart from removing the hyperlinks to GIFs of Lady Kluck from the Disney Robin Hood. GIFs of Lady Kluck are what the internet is for – go there if you need them.

WEDNESDAY 15TH APRIL 2015:

What does "hingmy" mean?
I hear it all the time in Glasgow

'Hingmy' *(aka hingmie)* means 'thing', and is often used when you can't find the right word, or you don't know the correct word. It's a combination of a variation on 'thing' and the suffix '-y' or '-ie' which is often used as a diminutive or to show familiarity. You often see it in names – eg. Anne to Annie, or Tom to Tommy. FUN FACT! That practice began first in Scotland as early as 1400, and spread south. SIDE FACT: at school my name, Ishbel, was always made into a pet name as 'Ishy', but when I went to university with predominantly English pals, they shortened my name to 'Ish'. I still have divided views on the nickname 'Ish' because I associate it with moving away from what I was used to, what I thought I'd chosen by studying in Scotland (*I was certainly the token Scot in my University of Edinburgh theatre-making crowd at Bedlam*). It's also associated with some of my best pals, though, so it's definitely mixed.

Back to hingmie. Here's an example sentence: 'Ma computer's been on the blink since A plugged in the USB hingmie'. Or: 'Turn that guff off, gie me the TV changer hingmie'. Variants include 'thingmy' and 'thingy'. That use of a 'h' sound where there would often be a 'th' sound in other dialects, and in other words in the speaker's dialect, applies elsewhere too eg. somehing = something. I have zero evidence for this, but it also feels like 'nuhin' is gaining ground while the older form, 'naethin' is losing it.

The word 'hingmie' is shockingly absent from the Concise Scots Dictionary, but 'thingy' makes it to the OED (*TOP TIP: pretty much any library card can get you into the OED online where you have free access to pure hunners o information – dae it!*). The OED identifies 'thingy' as a chiefly Scottish word, which I had no idea about until RIGHT NOW. Added to the information about that '-y'/-'ie' suffix starting in Scotland, it's not so surprising.

This is a fair fascinatin wee hingmie, daein this here blog.

THURSDAY 16TH APRIL 2015:

Have you encountered people who say Scots is "slang?" How would you answer it?

First question answer: yup.

Second question answer: in the words of Johann Wolfgang Unger I, 'mitigate, hesitate and negatively predicate Scots even while saying how important it is to [me]'.

When I was rehearsing *Hoolet*, I took my watch in to the shoe/watch repair place near my flat. The guy in there asked me whether I was off work that day. This a perennial question for freelancers who can do things like go to the bank in office hours. I sometimes just say that it's my day off rather than explaining my complex work situation. But sometimes I get defensive about not being busy enough, because my self-esteem is pinned on whether someone I see every five months or so to pay in a cheque from my granny thinks I have a valid job. Oi.

Anyway, I explained to the guy in the shop that I was rehearsing a show. Here's how it went from there:

MAN: Oh yeah? What's the show aboot?

ISHBEL: It's about Scots language? *[the rising inflection of question is important here]*

MAN: Oh right, like Gaelic.

ISHBEL: N-no. Like, like if you use the word hoose instead of house, you could call that Scots.

MAN: Right, like a sortae slang.

ISHBEL: Well, you could call it a slang, but it has a long history *[mumbles]* and so I would call it a language.

MAN: *[He's got it now]* Yeah, sortae old-timey language.

ISHBEL: Well, people still speak it now. I suppose that's what the show's… *[trails off]*

MAN: That's me done. I tightened up that second hand, it was a bit shoogly. That's £4.80.

ISHBEL: Thanks so much. That's great. Can I pay by card?

MAN: Aye. *[Gets out chip and pin machine]* Ye know, A get charged aboot 15p for usin this, an 40p or somehin fir usin it under a fiver.

ISHBEL: Oh, right, I'm *[she means 'awkward', but can't say it]* – do you want to add that? *[This last section is too quiet to really hear]*

MAN: Nae worries. Yer nearly at a fiver. Ither fowk though…

[The conversation continues until Ishbel awkwardly leaves, smiling and apologising with her whole body]

> To me, that man is a Scots speaker. Does he see his language as a slang? Does he see himself as just speaking English? What difference would it make to his life just now if I was to have taken the time to try and explain to him the history and validity of his idiolect? Would that have been more or less annoying than me paying by card?

> BOY, DO I NOT KNOW.

THURSDAY 16TH APRIL 2015:

When will I be able to write
a job application in Scots?

Pretty sure by the end of the run *(25th April 2015)* the whole Scots language issue should be over, so sometime early in May you should be able to apply to Morgan Stanley in Scots no bother.

Ha.

Yeah. This is a tough one. Triple threat:

1. written

2. job

3. application

Let's go through them one by one.

ONE: WRITTEN – We're still not used to seeing Scots written. Indeed, it bothers us that there is little standardisation in the spelling when we do see it. At times like in job applications, we tend to take good spelling, punctuation and grammar, and a formal style, as a mark of the suitability of that person for the job. We even take it as a mark of good character, even if the job will involve none of those skills. When it is hard to decide whether someone has done all of the writing 'right' because 'right' is unclear, we get all CAN'T PUT IN BOX HATE IT that humans do about so many different things.

TWO: JOB – We still think of spoken Standard English as the language of the workplace. And maybe it is. Or maybe it is in a general sense. It's not 'correct' Standard English to say 'me and Jesse are going to the shops', but it is PERFECTLY ACCEPTABLE in spoken language, since it is clear what you mean. If someone *speaks* like they would *write* in a formal situation, we would find them pretty odd.

There is an argument that it is alright to have different linguistic registers for different areas of our lives. Maybe in a lawyers' office with people from all over Britain, Europe and the world it makes sense to use English as a lingua franca. Lingua francas are useful, they've been used for as long as we've had language and people to talk to who aren't our family. There are arguments that English itself began as a sort of pidgin language or creole when Anglo-Saxon, French and Norse were jumbled together in the 11th century. Such creoles can be used as a lingua franca, and in this case *(if you accept this theory, which MILLIONS WOULDN'T)* came to dominate and take over the other languages it was bridging, namely French, Norse and Anglo-Saxon.

For me, the problem is when you say the language we use in the office is superior to the language we use at home. The hierarchy, rather than differentiation, is the issue. I don't know if we can sort that, though. If there's something that humans like it's putting things in order of bestness. So tactical use of the Scots language use in formal settings is a noble act which I applaud. However, it takes nerves of steel, especially if it's an application…

THREE: APPLICATION – The 'application' aspect of this suggestion makes everything more difficult. When we send an application for a job, or similar, the reader of that application only has that to go on. In a way, our instinct in a setting like a written application is for the form of the language to disappear, and for only the content to shine through. It's like how the mark of a good theatre technician is that no-one even noticed that they had done any job at all. Crushing. Standard English is so normative that it is seen as 'neutral'. When we are introducing ourselves as a good option for company money, we don't want to appear stupid, but also not flashy.

To send a job application in Scots, with no personality, reasoning, and apologetic shoulders to balance it, is an act of supreme bravery. And one that I have attempted ONCE in my life, and that was the award application for this show *(so doesn't quite count)*. I offered an English translation 'on request', but then sat in my room worrying that they wouldn't bother with the extra effort of reading an application in Scots and would take it as an easy way to slim down the pile. I thought about how if they did that I wouldn't want their money anyway. Then I thought about how I really wanted their money. Why was I making my life difficult when I knew how to make it easy? This is my first funded show as lead artist, and the topic is important to me. I wanted to have a chance to make the show and put it in front of people.

Eventually, I chickened out and asked the woman who was organising the application process if I should provide an English translation. She thought I should send one in, in case the panel needed it on the one day they would have to bash through them all. I really have no idea if they used the English or the Scots application.

So, when will you be able to write a job application in Scots? In some cases, now, but sharpen your nerves of steel first. And maybe resign yourself to the consequences. The more people do it, the more normal it will become, the more that won't be the one defining characteristic about you. Like early women who went to university: maybe you're going to have a tough time in your life, not being or doing what people expect, but future generations will be grateful that you took those risks, even though you often suffer as a result. Looking round my Senior Honours courses at uni I could count the number of men in my classes on one hand. Women women women. But in the Scots poetry class, no-one could read those poems aloud in Scots. Just. Not. Physically. Capable.

Maybe the answer to the question is never? When will we hear a newsreader use the word 'hoose' instead of house from behind the newsroom desk? My lifetime? Or nevertime?

MAK IT NOO, FOWK. MAK IT NOO/ MAK IT NEW.

THURSDAY 16TH APRIL 2015:

What is the literal translation of 'hoots'?

'Hoots' or 'hoot', in the words of the OED, seems to be a 'natural utterance of objection or revulsion'. I am delighted by this natural utterance. The Concise Scots Dictionary describes it as 'expressing dissent, incredulity, impatience, annoyance, remonstrance or dismissal of another person's opinion'. In English you might say an equivalent is 'tut', or maybe 'tush'. There are similar sounds of disapproval in Swedish *(hut begone,* used in taking one up sharply), Welsh *(hwt* off! away!), Irish *(ut* out! pshaw!), Gaelic *(ut! ut!* interj. of disapprobation or dislike).

An additionally delightful thing is that the OED thinks that hoot as an interjection might have originally been an attempt to echo the sound of hoolets! The vowel sound *u* is heard at the furthest distances, so hoot sounds, or 'hoo', or 'ooohoo' are often used in calls. The Middle English *hūten* is found from *c*1200, for example. Coooooool!

THURSDAY 16TH APRIL 2015:

How old is Scots language?

This question is quite difficult to answer about any language. How old is English language? Language exists on a spectrum – it is hard to identify when one language ends and one begins geographically, historically, linguistically. That is so much a part of the problem that Scots has – can we and should we define the moment when some spoken or written Standard Scottish English 'becomes' Scots? The same is true historically – when does Anglo-Saxon, the common ancestor between modern Scots and English, 'become' Scots or English?

The Anglo-Saxon language came to Scotland in the seventh century AD. So in one sense, we could say that Scots began then. The seventh century is certainly an important date in its history. But is that Scots? A problem that we have when looking into whether that was indeed 'Scots' is that Anglo-Saxon is also sometimes called Old English. So many people will say that the language spoken then was English. But if 'Old English' conjures up images of men in breeches and Shakespeare for you, think again. Here is the start of the most famous piece of Anglo-Saxon literature, *Beowulf*, written down:

Hwæt. We Gardena in geardagum,
þeodcyninga, þrym gefrunon,
hu ða æþelingas ellen fremedon.
Oft Scyld Scefing sceaþena þreatum,
monegum mægþum, meodosetla ofteah,
egsode eorlas. Syððan ærest wearð
feasceaft funden, he þæs frofre gebad,
weox under wolcnum, weorðmyndum þah,
oðþæt him æghwylc þara ymbsittendra
ofer hronrade hyran scolde,
gomban gyldan. þæt wæs god cyning.

Now, sometimes different languages LOOK very different but when you hear them you can totally hear the connections, or understand the gist. You often get that with 15th or 16th century Scots – looks impenetrable but spoken can often sound much more recognisable. Yeah. Not with Anglo-Saxon/Old English. When I hear it spoken I think: isn't it lovely? Isn't it not English?

The Anglo-Saxon language spread from the south east of Scotland and over about 400 years embedded itself in the lower parts of Scotland – the Borders, east coast, north east, Caithness area and Northern Isles. Part of its spread was due to conscious displacement by David I of Gaelic speakers in the new burgh towns, so the language of power became that Anglic language. Many Gaelic speakers learned the powerful language; the Gaelic language retreated slightly. But the higher land continued to be dominated by Gaelic, much, much more widespread than it has been in living memory. For example, Kinross, where I'm from, is solidly lowland *(biggest loch in the Lowlands, lads)* but the name – from Gaelic ceann + ros – shows that it was once Gaelic speaking. So tell anyone having a go at the Gaelic place names on station signage to (LOWLAND) PIPE(*S*) DOWN.

The question of the age of Scots is not made easier by the fact that early speakers of the Scots-ancestor-language referred to themselves as 'Inglis', or English, speakers. In, say, the 12th century, 'Scottis' referred to the ancestor of what we now call Gaelic. The first person we know of to use the word 'Scottis' to refer to the Anglic language that we now call Scots was Gavin Douglas, a poet and cleric born in the 15th century. He was referring to the translation he did of Virgil's *Aeneid* into Scots, *Eneados* – the first translation of any major Latin or Greek secular text into any Anglic language. Douglas, fairly uniquely for the time, set up a contrast between 'Scottis' and 'suddron', the language of England. Fun fact! *Eneados* is the first ever citing of the word 'scone' in the OED.

Maybe we date Scots from the moment that a modern, contemporary Scots speaker would be able to get by with a historical speaker. In that case there's certainly a case that a 15th/16th century speaker like Douglas or Dunbar would be able to get by with a current inhabitant of Easterhoose. But would they get by differently with a Standard English speaker? Because Scots has been relatively more conservative than English, would a Scots speaker do better with a fourteenth century 'suddron' speaker like Chaucer than a twenty-first century Standard

English speaker would? And if so, WHAT DOES THAT MEAN?

Yeah. Complicated.

Basically: Scots is older than a lot of people think. If its age gives it weight for those who think of it as a poor debasement of modern English, then send them here to me and I will complicate this even more for them. Mary Beard, the Roman historian, and I are in agreement on many points. And now, using her words, I stand to say: "What is the role of an academic, no matter what they're teaching, within political debate? It has to be that they make issues more complicated. The role of the academic is to make everything less simple."

Sorry, not sorry.

SATURDAY 23RD APRIL 2016:

Do you spell jobbie(y) with a ie or a y?

I did my Masters at drama school in Glasgow with many English and American students. We were pally with the undergraduate actors and, while hanging out with them, it became clear that one of my classmates had never heard the word 'jobby'. This shocked the English and American undergraduate actors. It seemed that their Scottish classmates used the word jobby roughly *(roughagely?)* five times a day. And why wouldn't you? It brings you all sorts of joy when people who don't know that in Scotland it means 'poo' use it to just mean 'a wee thing': 'Will you hand me the blue jobbie for the carrots?'; 'I think you get a special jobbie to fix that bit of a bike'. Etc.

To answer the question, though, I have used the spellings that the OED prefers above: 'jobbY' for poo; 'jobbIE' for small job, or object that does a job, or even a place.

BUT, one of those things that is great about writing this blog, I discovered that according to the OED, the use of 'jobby' for poo is, wait for it, AMERICAN – first recorded in 1981. And sure enough, the first recording that the Scots Language Dictionary has for that usage is as late as 1989. I am SHOCKED. Also the quotation they have from the corpus for the first Scots use of 'jobby' gies me the dry boaks.

FOR FURTHER INTEREST on the Y versus IE stuff, have a look at my other blog post on the meaning of the word 'higmy'.

Why are street names being replaced in Gaelic and not "Scots" language especially in the south where gaelic was never spoken.

This is a question that I have had a good few times on the tour, and it's one that I have heard many times in my life. Out in the world this question is not usually asking why Gaelic and not Scots, but why Gaelic at all. Having an employer mouthing off about the 'waste of money' that was Gaelic signage *('nobody speaks it', 'it's dead already' etc etc)*, was once part of my reason for leaving a job. I wish I had the sort of job where you have interviews, so that when I had an interview for my next job and they said, 'Why did you leave your last place?' I could say, 'Linguistic narrow-mindedness.'

But there is a strong discussion to be had about Gaelic vs. Scots signage. There has been a 'traditional' view of Gaelic being north and west of the Highland line, and Scots everywhere else. So the argument runs that there should only be Gaelic on street signage or train stations in the Highlands and Islands. This word 'traditional' is tricky, though. Traditional since when? Scotland has been multi-lingual since writing began. Are we going from when the Romans arrived to write about it? There was the Brythonic language varieties which were very close to Welsh that dominated the southern part of Scotland at that time. There was Pictish *(find any evidence of the nature of that language and you will be an Academic Monarch)*. There were Norse languages which held on in Shetland, Orkney and Caithness, there was English, there was Scots, there was Gaelic. But English was Inglis and might have been Scots, Scots was Gaelic, or Irish was Gaelic and Scots was named as a political act. I talked about this conglomeration of confusion in my How old is Scots Language? post. The truth is, many of these areas which we think of as not at all Gaelic-speaking, but strong, Scots-speaking heartland, were areas which were forced to abandon their culture and language in favour of Scots a few hundred years ago. There is an excellent summary of Scottish history on the Quora website *(REMEMBER: never read the bottom half of the internet)*, and one of the things it emphasises is that the Kingdom of Scotland was expansionist. Many areas where we are angry about the use of Gaelic on signage are not Gaelic speaking because the folk in those areas were forced by sword, gun and grain to speak English. Also known as Scots. Here's a classic from the Quora article:

In 1609, for example, the Scottish government passed a law (the Statutes of Iona) requiring Highland clan chiefs to send their sons to school in the Scottish Lowlands where they could learn English ('Inglishe'), so that: "the Irish language [ie, Gaelic] which is one of the chief and principal causes of the continuance of barbarity and uncivilised behaviour ['incivilitie'] among the inhabitants of the Isles and Highlands, may be abolished and removed".

And even not going back that far, the last speaker of Perthshire Gaelic died in living memory. Does that mean Gaelic signage is okay in Perthshire? That woman was alive with people who were alive with people who were alive with Gaelic in many other areas of Scotland. My home town, Kinross, has a Gaelic name – *Ceann Ros*, head of the point. But my home, Burnbrae, is Scots – the house up from the wee river. Not only have places been a mish-mash historically, but now there are many Gaelic speakers in, say, Edinburgh. There is a Gaelic medium school in Leith, and two in Glasgow. There are Scots speakers on the Isle of Coll, or Lewis, or in Ullapool. We move. To say that on our signage, a thing which we erect to help people navigate, we will have only the languages 'spoken' in that area is like when you arrive in a strange town and the taxi company advertises its phone number in the train station without the area code. This is only for folk around here. Worse than that, it's like implying that Gaelic speakers don't travel out of the Gàidhealtachd, or that they only deserve to see their language in that bubble.

So. Gaelic was spoken more places than you think. Scots is spoken more places than you think. Nobody worries about English on signs. Have all three. Language visibility is important. And if you want to see Scots signage in reality, heid awa tae Keith. Ploo Lane! Sodger Lane! It's braw! The future, ladies and gentlemen! The future!

FRIDAY 10TH JUNE 2016:

Link between language and songs.

Oh boy. Audiences. You don't pull your punches, do you?

This question has innumerable PhDs of stuff to say. I am going to talk about Scots language in song.

Let's start with a couple of nots: I am not going to talk about the link between language and music. But boy is that deep. And maybe I will end up talking about it a bit. Who can say? This is a magical mystery tour! I'm a passenger as much as you! Wait. Who's driving?

I am not going to go into loads of detail on the Proper Science research that *Hoolet's* Creative Learning leader, Dr Michael Dempster, has done on this subject. Mostly because my understanding is predominantly 'oh, it's so cool, basically he's found these things that are like Scots but in music form and I don't remember them or anything else about them but it's really cool.'

So. Scots in Song.

Song is one of those places where Scots has managed to stay acceptable. Poetry is similar. Some reasons why I think Scots is more acceptable in song than in other situations.

1. Robert Burns – Scotland's most successful writer and Top Export sort of _is_ the Scots language for many people. Auld Lang Syne caught the world at the start of mass culture and became everyone's national song. Apparently in China they think it is a native Chinese song. Scots is safe, poetic and couthie in song. It is like singing hymns with 'thee' and 'thou' in – not really okay for life, but jolly good fun with a rousing, Victorian tune. Saying that, it doesn't mean that people necessarily sing the Scots songs in a very Scots way. Even Eddi Reader Anglicises/Americanises when she's singing Burns. Not Mairi Campbell in the _Sex and the City_ movie though. What a champ. Anyway. Off point. Or is it?

2. Anglicisation of Scots in song – Maybe one of the reasons Scots is easier in song is precisely because you don't have to have a Scots accent to sing it. Given that we sing all pop songs with American accents, and English people sing folk with a West Country accent, or the New Folk lot all sound like they come from South London via private school *(for all three you can go to Laura Marling)*. For a great chat about Multilingual identity in song, have a look at 'Lisa Loves Linguistics' talking about Rihanna. Scots has long been considered fine in song. It's safe, it's local, it's folk.

3. Song is oral – We are much more likely to learn a song by ear than other forms of culture. We learn them orally even from recordings. I can recreate every sound in Cerys Matthews' voice in *International Velvet*. I've never looked at the words, as evidenced in the fact that I am often singing the sounds with no link to meaning – 'if you'd sinis bot and ickalinnin'. Even the Welsh. Print likes to standardise, the ear doesn't mind quite so much. *(PS. What is his 'godforsaken soy?')*

4. Old Scots is safe Scots – Most of the Scots songs that are performed and heard in 2016 are well over a century or more old. The Proclaimers have sung eloquently on the subject of not even being allowed a Scottish accent in contemporary music. Maybe that means Scots is not as safe in

songs as I think? Isobel McArthur doesn't feel it's safe in her show, *How to Sing It* which investigates the struggles and richness of accent diversity within her one voice.

I'm giving up the bullet points. Too many reasons and too few. One thing I feel is certain, if Scots has any clout as a language, it is in large part due to song, which has validated it, protected it, passed it on, and enlivened it.

Thank you, song.

FRIDAY 10TH JUNE 2016:

It's a very polite language – what are their good bad words? Cussin' words

Very polite? I am really interested in this question as I think it highlights that old Caldonian Antisyzygy – the idea that our concept of Scottishness is split between raving Celt and Presbyterian minister. Or in this case, maybe the two stereotypes of Scots language I am thinking of are:

1. Gorbals hard man, who makes even English sound like a threat. See the below extract from the 'Xenophobes Guide to Scots':

However, Scottish accents vary greatly around the country. From the mouth of a

Glaswegian, for instance, a declaration of love can sound like a death threat. From the native of a Hebridean island, a death threat can sound like poetry. Strangely enough the accents all sound Scottish *(even the Aberdonians, and not even the Scots understand what they are saying)*.

2. Shortbread tin, Harry Lauder Scots of Och Aye The Noo and the Queen at Balmoral.

It seems that the questioner was thinking more about number 2 and I was thinking more about number 1. Which says somethings about both of us, I'm sure.

As for good swearwords in Scots, we share a lot of our swearwords with English because their origins seem to be older than the split of Anglo Saxon into Scots and English. If you want to fill up on swear word facts, have a listen to Helen Zaltzman's excellent Allusionist podcast episode on 'Detonating the C-Bomb'. NOT SAFE FOR BROADCASTING IN THE WORK PLACE OR WITH CHILDREN OR GRANNIES.

Purely Scots swearwords? Keech *(shit)* is good. Relatively light, but to the anatomical point is the word 'bawbag'. In fact, it's light enough to be a range of boxers and the name for a hurricane of 2011 that meant the Met Office had to start giving the hurricanes names like 'Abigail' and 'Barney'. There's also the other side of the swaery coin where the C-Word as detonated in Helen's podcast is not nearly as strong in many Scots situations. You can, for example, legitimately refer to a friend as a 'great cunt'. I think it still has some welly, though, when thrown aggressively (*like I clearly never do – I just referred to the impact of the most aggressive swearword in English as having 'some welly'*).

There's 'fanny', or, more specifically, 'ya fanny'. It makes listening to Americans being prim in American English and incredibly rude in the UK deeply funny. Need a pack for your fanny? Or a pack for fannies in general? They got it. At my primary school the strongest swearword was 'fud' which was female genitals or pubes. I remember once asking other Scottish people not from Kinross Primary if they knew the word, and they'd never heard of it. I don't need confirmation from RL people when I have the dictionary, though. Sure enough it's 'coarse slang'. I love dictionaries, they are true friends.

The more I think about the lack of Scots swearwords in the public sphere, the more I wonder if it is because the people we see writing in Scots are people like me – middle class, uni educated, liberal cunts. We don't tend to use sweary words anyway. Hmm.

Also, there's the issue of translating sociolinguistics between social groups. Hearing that in some foreign country it's a huge insult to say someone has dirty ears, or whatever, is quaint. So maybe the swearwords of other groups just sound polite because you've not been brought up with the taboo around them. My phone still thinks I often want to 'duck it'. And why not? Phones don't know that a few different letters take it from VERY BAD to NICE AQUATIC BIRDS *(though ducks are mega-rapists…)*. FUN STORY! The BSL signs for lemonade and fuck are the same hand movements. You identify which you mean by facial expression and context. While learning the word for lemonade in isolation, though, and with a face that was screwed up in concentration, my husband was told off by our teacher for being a VERY BAD BOY.

Ultimately, my strongest swearword is 'chum'. If I use it as a noun with you, be very afraid. I'll chum you somewhere, no bother. But if you have accelerated from the lights too fast when I am crossing the road, you will get an 'Alright, chum'. And I'd mean it too.

Haar – Scots? For mist [...] origin?

What. A. Great. Word.

This is definitely a contender for my favourite Scots word – a question I get asked pretty frequently in the show.

Haar is the cold, wet, sea mist that can flood Edinburgh, even when two miles inland it's glorious sunshine. It doesn't just apply to Edinburgh, anywhere on the East Coast, but I associate it with being a student in the capital because we didn't get any such thing in Kinross, which was Very Inland For Scotland *(ie. 30 minutes from the sea)*. We never get it in Glasgow either. In Scarborough, in the north east of England, they call it the 'fret' and it is spectacular.

The word is not exclusively Scots, it's used all along the east coast from north of Lincolnshire. The origin is the Middle Dutch word 'hare', which meant a 'keen cold wind'.

Maybe my connection of haar with Edinburgh isn't only personal. The misty, mysteriousness that the haar brings to the Old Town is part of what gives it its ghostly, medieval character.

The haar made Edinburgh, like the Clyde made Glasgow.

PS: I had a friend who was in a progressive black metal band in Edinburgh called Haar. I went to see them in a gig once and I wore a little, flowery dress and my fluffy blonde hair in pleats. I fitted right in.

SUNDAY 21ST AUGUST 2016:

Is Scots grammar different from English? (And other languages?) (Eg. "I'm away" is present but used for future = going away)

Yup.

There are plenty of interesting grammatical features of Scots. They tend to be seen as much less acceptable than differences of vocab. I suppose because we all have grammar hardwired into the brain *(if you don't agree, take it up with Chomsky)*, we can't help but feel other people's grammars are incorrect. It is hard to believe that in some areas of the West Country in England, it is grammatical to conjugate 'to be' as:

I am
you am
he/she/it am

But it IS grammatical. It is grammatical in Scots to use the double modal, for example: 'I'll can come on Tuesday', meaning 'I am able to come on Tuesday'. The use of 'will' and 'can' together, both modal verbs, is not grammatical in Standard English, but it is in Scots.

The best way to learn about the differences between Scots and Standard English grammar is to take a look at two excellent books: *Modren Scots Grammar* by Christine Robinson, and *A Scots Grammar* by David Purves. If you want a work-book, have a go at *Grammar Broonie* by the excellent Matthew Fitt. It's fun to even skim through any of those books and go, 'Oh yeah! I recognise that! Here's me thinking 'here's me' was ungrammatical.'

The following is the text for a short performance I did at the launch of the second edition of the *Concise Scots Dictionary*. It was written specifically for an audience of dictionary fans and lexicographers (dream audience) and was only ever performed that one time, with my dad as my assistant.

Concise Scots Stories
– Ishbel McFarlane, December 2017

Some of youse micht hae seen ma shaw, *O is for Hoolet*, whaur A explore Scots wi the yaise o nummert questions. A've been daein it that long that noo A fund A cannae perform wi oot nummers. A'm gonnae hae ma faither hud up signs an A'd like ye tae read the nummer oot lood. They're scrievit in Scots but ye can say them in whitever leid ye prefer – extra pynts fir Pictish – an fir ilk nummer A'll gie ye a concise Scots story fir the Concise Scots Dictionary. We'll hae a practice:

Okay dokey?

AYE
Richt, we're aff.

ANE
The ainly ither time A've bin at a Dictionar launch, wis when A wis aboot ten year auld. Ma mither an faither kent Iseabail Macleod an she hid bin warkin oan the Scots School Dictionary. Iseabail Macleod wis the ainly ither Ishbel A'd

iver met. A mind there wis food, an a chance fir ma mither and faither tae speak wi smert fowk, while A hid a shot oan the door's entry buzzer.

It cam tae the launch pairt, an awbody gaithert roon, an A stood wi ma faither wha pit his hauns oan ma shouthers. Some gadgie welcomed awbody and congratulatit the lexicographers oan their wark and then he said, 'Now Ishbel is going to come up and say a few words'. Ma faither says A physically jamp.

But in ma heid A thocht, 'Okay, A'll dae ma best'.

TWA

A bairn is sittin in the Salutation Hotel in Perth waitin fir their turn in a Burns competition. They hae a wee sheet wi the order o the contestants oan it. Ivry time they see thir name printit there, they get a wee thrill. Tae hae somehing that close, tae see it, in black printit letters, official – it's electric.

OR

Whan A wis a child nerd, A took pairt in Burns festivals. A mind sittin in the Salutation Hotel in Perth an luikin at the schedule an seein ma name printit oan the competitor list. Tae hae somehin that close tae me, tae see it, in black printit letters, it sent a thrill frae ma taes tae ma heid.

THREE

The BSL sign for language is *[signs]* LANGUAGE

FOWER

Three fowk is in a room in Friesland, in the Netherlands, talkin aboot Friesian – twa o the fowk is Friesian speakers an ane is a Scots speaker. The three fowk yaise English as their lingua franca. They speak aboot the connections atween the twa minority leids. The Scots spikker lauchs whan she hears that Frisian fir exit is utgong.

The Friesian spikkers talk o the triligual nurseries in their toon, whaur bairns learn Dutch, Friesian an English. They talk o hoo whan ye phone the emergency services in Friesland, ye can chaise tae speak wi a Friesian spikker, cause yer no wantin tae hae tae hink aboot yer leid whan it's bad eneuch tae call the emergency services.

The Scots speaker says 'There's no way to learn Scots in Scotland, in an evening class or whatever.' An the Friesian speakers say, 'What?' The Scots speaker says, 'You can't do an evening class in Scots, like you could do with Italian or French. They don't exist in Scotland'. An the Friesian speakers say, 'What?'

FIVE

Limmy, aka Brian Limmond, is a Scottish comedian frae Glesga. He his twa Scottish Baftas fir his BBC sketch shaw. His sketches is hilarious, weird and is sometimes that close tae the bone ye cannae watch.

Here's the douce stert o ane o his sketches:

Aw right? Dye want tae know why A'm smilin? Aw right. Come ere an A'll let ye in a wee secret. Just bought maself a new pair o socks. No jist any kind o socks, no the kind o socks ye buy in a pack o five fir a couple o quid – naw – A'm talkin about the kinda socks that make ye go lu that, 'Pffffff no peyin that fir a pair o socks.'

SAX

The BSL sign for interrupt is *[signs]* INTERRUPT

SEIVEN

Twa lads is fechtin in a classroom in Perth an ane o the laddies shouts, 'A'll kick yer **airse!**' an a passin teacher chastises, 'David Mackay!' an David Mackay immediately apologises, 'Sorry sir, arse.'

ECHT

Whan A wis in Copenhagen last month A got the bus intae the Danish Royal Library, whaur A wis researchin Scots, Gaelic an British Sign Leid. A dae ken onie Danish, an this wis ma first trip oan the bus, so A sat masel on the first seat A cuid fund – no wantin tae luik oot o place, lik A didnae belang.

A wee whilie intae the journey frae Nørrebro, what the Danes pronounce No-bo, an auld mannie is staunnin waitin oan tae share ma seat, an richt eneuch A suddenly see the sign that says it's ane thit's meant fir folk wi disabilities or that. A shoogled ma wey alang the double seat an he sat next tae me. A apologised an did a lot o ma usual smiling and nodding, an he did the same, talkin tae me in Danish A didnae unnerstaun.

He paused his talkin an pit his haun in his pooch an held oot his haund palm doon, lik that, tae gie me something. A said, 'No, no. Thank you' gesturing. As A gestured he took ma haun an pit in it a sweetie. A smiled an A said 'thank you', but A'm allergic tae a wheen o things an no aw sweeties are suitable fir me an so A kept it in ma haun as the wheels oan the bus went roon an roon.

He spak an A listened, daein the same smilin an noddin, until he asked a question an held up his finger: ane. A cuid tell he wis checkin tae see if A'd unnerstood. But A didnae, an the ainly thing A cuid think tae dae wis tae yaise the British Sign Language sign for 'I cannae mind', because een in BSL A dae ken hoo tae say 'I dae unnerstaund'.

He laughed, an he took ma haun again, an A thocht he wantit tae shake it, so A shook his, but he took ma haun an the sweetie and pit it tae ma mooth: eat it. It's fir you. Rude noo, A still didnae eat it, but I cupped it an A bowed.

An we sat thegither fir the twenty minute journey. A luikit oot the windae, an ivvry noo an then he'd speak again, an A wis stuck again, in ma kenlessness. But slowly A gaithered that he wis Polish, an the next word I kent is Siberia. Five fingers, five years, Siberia. Mmmhmm, An A'm sayin 'Ooooh, cooold, Haaard.'

An we pause.

An then A think he's asking where I am from. An A say, 'Scotland' and he goes hmm? An he pits his lug richt by ma moo an A shout tae the bus an ma freen, SCOTLAND. An he goes, Aaaaaah! *[mimes] SKIRT*, which wad seem reductive gin the BSL fir Scotland wisnae *[signs SCOTLAND] BAGPIPES*. After *[mimes] SKIRT* he shows *[mimes] MUSCLES* and A'm that pleased and A say, 'Aye aye! Yes yes! Scotland'

An we pause.

An then he's askin me mair an A get naethin until he says: Scotland you speak English. An A say, *[pause]* 'Yes', decidin no tae get intae it the noo. An he says Scotland *[holds up one hand]* an then England *[holds up other hand]* and he grabs, an claps an shoves an A cannae guess wha's fechters and wha's victims, but A nod.

An A stert tae realise that some o his words is German. An he sterts on Poland again, an he taks his finger an he draws on the back o the seat in front o him POLAND, and then he draws a line through it, an he grabs ae side RUSKIS and he grabs the ither side an he sis DEUTCHLAND. An then he asks what A think is 'Do you speak Russian?' an A reply No. Sorry.

Addin tae the list o leids A cannae speak.

NINE

Ma stage manager fir ma shaw aboot Scots, *O is for Hoolet*, organised Limmy's book tour. She's tellin him aboot *Hoolet*, an hoo he'd like it cause he yaises Scots an aw, an he says, 'Aye, but s'no like thir's a dictionary in it or that.'

TEN

Whan A went tae Buckie wi *O is for Hoolet*, fowk spak Scots tae me whan they didnae ken me – in shops, oan the street, een the official-luikin wifie at the post office – A wis amazed. Growin up in Kinross, and steyin in Embrae, that didnae happen. Een in Glesga A dae get it that much. A thocht o a fantasy land in the North East whaur ye cuid hae Scots immersion.

ELEIVEN

The second maist common audience question A get aboot Scots is 'Is baffies a word? My family use it to mean slippers'.

TWAL

The singl worst mark A ivver got at the University o Edinburgh was fir an essay oan Scots Language marked bi Chris Robinson.

THIRTEEN

Limmy's maist mainstream appearance oan TV wis whan he wis oan the London-made shaw *The IT Crowd*. In it he pleyed a windae cleaner that cuildnae be unnerstuid on accoont o bein Glaswegian.

FOWERTEEN

Sin October A've bin daein wark in Kelty, Crossgates an Hill o Beath – aw in Fife. Wi busy traffic ootside the garden centre, Kelty is an eleven minute drive frae ma childhood hame.

A stertit ma wark wi a performance o ma interactive shaw, *Plan*, whaur the audience hae a chance tae build a toon frae scratch – they mak ivvry decision, frae hoo mony hooses, tae whether tae hae ferms, or a baths, or schuils, een tae hoo the place will luik. The kids frae Beath High loved chaisin their hings fir the toon, but didnae gie twa hoots aboot hoo the place luikit.

Ae boy hid bin sayin 'KELTY KELTY KELTY'
in the pandemonium that filled the haw. A asked,
'Are you from Kelty? Do you think that the town
that you've made looks like Kelty'

Kelty's shite, ken? But this place disnae luik
onyhing like Kelty, sae it must be shiter.

FIFTEEN
The BSL sign for thank you is *[signs]* THANK-
YOU

SIXTEEN
The BSL sign for sorry is *[signs]* SORRY

SEVENTEEN
The Scots for thank you is 'sorry'

ECHTEEN
The BSL sign for start is *[signs]* START

NINETEEN
The BSL sign for start again is *[signs]* START
AGAIN

TWENTY
The BSL sign for start again now is *[signs]*
START AGAIN NOW

'A passionate call to arms for the study
and preservation of minority languages.' *The Times* ★ ★ ★ ★

Language is personal. Nothing gets closer to our hearts. And yet, b
its own nature, it's always social. Who owns it? Who appoints it? Wh
governs it? And why?

In this one-woman show about the Scots language, Ishbel McFarlan
presents collected fragments – stories, interviews, memorie
characters and attitudes – to challenge and disrupt our expectation
and prejudices about language. By interrogating the history of Scot
and the ways in which it is taught and subdued, the audience is invite
to question the way forward for minority languages. Winner of Th
Arches Platform 18: New Directions Award 2014.

Includes extra bonus questions and *Concise Scots Stories*, a one
off performance commissioned for the *Concise Scots Dictionar*
book launch.

'A witty, intelligent, and interesting discussion on the subject of language
Darrow ★ ★ ★ ★

'An engaging, heart-warming piece which is a lovingly made look at
language as a living, pulsating, external thing as natural as breathing.'
The List ★ ★ ★ ★

Ishbel McFarlane is a performer, writer and theatre maker from Kinross, no
in Glasgow, via Edinburgh. She makes work which focuses on social justic
feminism, place, history and language.

ISBN 978-1-913630-12-6

9 781913 630126

51595

£12.99 / $17.95
SALAMANDERSTREET.COM
PLAYS

DAN O'BRIEN

THE
ANGEL
IN
THE
TREES

and Other Monologues